The Secret Art of Mead Making Revealed

Will Kalif

CONTENTS

Will Kalif

INTRODUCTION

Congratulations!

You are about to embark on a wonderful adventure that is steeped in very old tradition. It is the secret art of mead making. Some believe is the oldest form of brewing -and they might be right.

And I call this the secret art of mead making because there really isn't a whole lot printed about it. And there is a bit of an irony here because there doesn't need to be a whole lot printed about it. Mead making is quite simple and a minimalist can make a successful batch with just honey, water and yeast. That is all that is really needed.

But of course there are a lot of details and variations and a lot of things you should do to insure a successful, and tasty, batch of mead. And this book is all about those things -demystifying the secret and giving all the basic rules and techniques that will insure you make some great mead and have some fun along the way.

I get email from people all the time telling me that they love medieval stuff and have always wanted to make some mead.

And the information found on my website (www.stormthecastle.com) gave them the knowledge and the confidence to give it a try! "Maybe it isn't so hard after all." Is what I imagine they always think to themselves? And they are right. It really isn't that hard.

If you are one of these people and you bought this book because you always wanted to actually make some mead yourself then I offer you a big congratulations! You are now on your way to making yourself some of the most ancient and delicious beverage ever made.

And don't be surprised if you are bitten by the bug and you start making more of it. This is what happened to me. I wanted to just taste some mead and I couldn't get any so I was forced to make my own. And now I have made more batches than I can count.

It is real easy to get very involved with mead because there are so many variations to try like pumpkin, apple, pear, cinnamon and well - you get the idea. If you have a favorite flavor or favorite fruit you are going to find yourself thinking about making a batch of mead with it. This is part of the real beauty of mead. It can be a blank palette that takes on many different flavors.

Have fun and be sure to send me an email telling me about your adventures in mead making!

What this book is

This book is a primer and guide that will give you a clear understanding of how to make mead. It is aimed at beginners who have never made mead before or people who have just begun.

I have kept everything clear and simple and I get you off to a fast start. I have kept out a lot of the complications that can be written about mead making because after all, mead is actually very easy to make.

With this book you will gain a good understanding of mead making and the courage to make it. I have de-mystified the secret. You will also learn a lot of the fundamental skills that will allow you to spread your wings and experiment on your own with mead making if you so desire.

This is a small book and that is by design. There are other books out there that will give you a lot of information – very useful information if you want to get serious about the art of mead making.

But the goal of this book is to give you the basics and to get you going fast in your quest to make some good mead successfully. It will give you a basic understanding of just about everything that is involved and the goal is to have you confident in no time at all and on your way to making mead.

If you make beer or wine

If you are already familiar with the process of making beer or grape wine you will no doubt be familiar with a lot of the process of mead making but there are some differences. Be aware of these differences and try to keep an empty glass when approaching mead making.

About the author and this book

I have been making mead for many years now and have done a lot of experimenting with yeast, flavorings, spices, sizes, and more. I have come up with some fantastic meads and I have had some enormous five gallon disasters.

I wrote this book to fill a need. Having had a mead website for a few years now I have received hundreds of emails from people who are just beginning out in their adventure of mead making (probably much as you are now doing) and are trying to understand the process of making mead.

It is this plethora of questions that inspired me to write this book. The questions have all been a tremendous help to me in understanding what the common concerns and obstacles are that a beginner has when making mead.

More help on the website

You probably have discovered this book through the Storm the Castle website. But if you are unaware of it I have a website with a very large section devoted to the art of mead making. There you can find all kinds of tutorials, recipes and lots of videos on the art and craft of mead making. You can even send me an email if you have any questions. You can find that section here: www.stormthecastle.com/mead/index.htm

You can also watch lots of mead making videos on my youtube channel at: http://www.youtube.com/user/epicfantasy

Never tasted mead?

Mead is a wine and it has some similarities to typical wines yet it is very different! If you have never tasted mead I highly recommend you get a couple of bottles and give it a try. I make this recommendation for a couple of reasons. First off you might not like it! It is like nothing you have ever tasted and only vaguely resembles traditional grape wine. Some people love it and other people don't like it at all.

So before you embark on your mead making journey you want to know that mead is something that you like. And secondly, if you have tasted mead before you will have a better sense of how your home made mead is doing.

And, because your first batch of mead will take almost a year before it is ready to drink you may want make up a quick batch of faux mead. This is just a mixture of white wine and honey. This will give you a semblance of what mead tastes like. I have the recipe for this in the Let's Make Some Mead section of this book.

1 ABOUT MEAD, HONEY, AND MEAD MAKING

The Art of Patience

One big rule applies to making mead – be patient! There are some fast recipes out there that will get you some mead reasonably quickly (a few weeks) but for the most part an average mead is going to take at least six months to a year before it gets to be drinkable and tasty.

This same rule of thumb applies to the making process of mead. It is slow to ferment and age. Tinkering with it can often be detrimental to the process. If you have questions about your mead while it is fermenting you should get some help before you start adding things to it or trying to fix it! It may not be broken!

How Mead is Made

Having read a lot of books on mead making I found it very difficult to understand exactly how to make it! This sounds like a contradiction because the books are about mead making. But what the issue here is that as a mead maker I know how to make mead and it would be very easy for me to make assumptions about what you as the reader know and understand about the art of making mead. So here is a short overview of the process. This is a great place to start if you know little or nothing about mead making.

There are three major steps in the mead making process. There is a primary ferment, a secondary ferment, and an aging. Once each step is complete you siphon the mead into a new container for its next step.

The Graphic above shows these three major steps.

Step One: Primary Ferment

In this step you mix up all your ingredients including water, honey, yeast and flavors or fruits. You typically do this in a food grade plastic fermentation pail. The pail has an airlock on it to release gases from the fermenting mead and typically all the ingredients stay in this pail from between 2 and 4 weeks.

It isn't mandatory that you use a fermentation pail for this process. You can use a glass carboy or jug but a pail is a little bit better. It keeps all light out of the ferment and it makes it a whole lot easier if you are adding fruit to your batch. The downfall to using a pail is the possibility of the plastic having an effect on the taste and smell of the mead – especially if the pail has been used many times and is heavily scratched. But this shouldn't be a concern if you are using a true food grade pail which is what they sell at home brewing shops.

Step Two: Secondary Ferment

Once the ferment has slowed down all of the liquid is siphoned into a glass carboy where it will spend a longer period of time. In this stage there is only the liquid. All of the sediment, fruit and other things have been left behind. The mead is still fermenting but at a very slow rate so this carboy also has an airlock.

This ferment period lasts between two and six months or even more. Note that there are a lot of successful variations in mead making and some recipes call for leaving the spices and fruit into the secondary ferment which is quite ok. Typically I remove all the fruit for the secondary ferment and this is what I recommend you do while you are a beginner. It reduces the risk of the flavor being too strong and it reduces the risk of the fruit going bad and contaminating the batch.

Step Three: Bottling and Aging

Once the secondary ferment is complete, the ferment process is done and the liquid is siphoned into wine bottles and corked. While the ferment will be complete the mead will still undergo aging. The time in this stage is typically very flexible and can even be indefinite. Typically you keep the mead bottled like this so the total time from the day you first started the batch is about a year. Then it is ready for drinking.

There are some things that you can do just before bottling including adding more honey or some sugar to it. This will cause a secondary ferment and turn your mead into a sparkling mead.

You also can add chemicals to it to stabilize, preserve, and prevent further fermentation. I cover these topics in this book.

Those are the three major steps in making mead. From there you have lots of different variations and lots of other things to do and I will be covering much of this as you progress though this book.

Flexibility in the Process

The process I have outlined here and in the rest of this book is one way to make mead. And you should know that there are lots of other ways to make it. For example some recipes will call for not adding any fruit or spices until the secondary ferment while other recipes will call for repeated stirring and adding of nutrients over the course of weeks.

You will run across a lot of variations in process when researching mead recipes and chances are good that they are all pretty good. Because after all when it comes down to it mead is just honey, water and yeast. Everything after that is flexible and variable.

So be confident in following a recipe as long as it has been done before. And let this be an encouragement to try your own process and way of making mead.

Making one or five gallon batches?

Traditionally people typically made 5-6 gallon batches and this is how a lot of the wine making industry is geared. But in the past few years, with the growing interest in mead making a lot of single gallon batches have been made and it seems to be a trend in the mead making hobby.

You can go either way but I recommend that if you are just beginning you start out with a one gallon batch. It will yield you about four standard bottles of wine. It will keep your initial expenses down and afford you the chance to learn and make mistakes.

Some important rules of thumb

Sanitation

This is very important and I can't stress it enough but sanitation is the single most important aspect of mead making. When you mix up your honey, water and possibly other ingredients you are creating an environment that is rich in nutrients -and unwanted bacteria or yeast will love it! If a stray or unwanted yeast gets into your mix it could prove disastrous to the mead. It could give it off flavors or even make it undrinkable.

You are pitching in a very large quantity of yeast cells (millions) and these will quickly take over the batch, which is a good thing but you really need to eliminate the chance of something unwanted taking hold of your batch. You do this by sanitizing everything very carefully. And I mean everything from the jugs to the utensils, thermometers, rubber corks, and anything else that will come into contact with the mead.

And sanitizing isn't the process of washing. It is the process of using some kind of chemical to kill anything unwanted.

It doesn't take long to do and it is well worth the effort to ensure you have a successful ferment. There are chemicals available that will do the job quickly, easily and safely. I will review these and explain how to use them.

• EasyClean- I use this all the time. It is inexpensive and easy to use. It is a commonly used chemical sanitizer for winemakers.

• Iodophor – This is an FDA approved contact sanitizer that contains iodine.

• Unscented Bleach - "about one tablespoon (1/2 fluid ounce, 15 ml) of typical unscented chlorine bleach per gallon of water is the maximum that should be used for sanitizing food contact surfaces, according to federal regulation".

• Wine supply shops will have plenty of various types of sanitizers that you can use.

Quality of Ingredients

When it comes to cooking you know that the outcome is very dependent upon the quality of the food you start with and this holds true for mead making which is a food too. So, do your best to use the highest quality ingredients that you can find or afford.

Honey – The quality of the honey affects the quality of your mead. Get the best honey you can afford. And the type of honey has an effect on the mead. Typically if you are making a plain mead you should use an orange blossom honey and if you are making a fruit mead (Melomel) you should use a clover honey. The Orange blossom honey adds a hint of flavor and scent to a plain mead. The clover honey is more of a blank palette that accepts the fruit and spice flavors better.

Honey Ratios in mead:
• Light mead: 2- 2 ½ pounds of honey per gallon of mead
• Medium mead: 3 pounds of honey per gallon of mead
• Heavy or Sack Mead: 4 pounds of honey per gallon of mead

To Boil or Not to Boil?

You can make a fine mead by either the boiling process or by not boiling. It tends to be a personal choice. I recommend you heat your honey and water mix to just below boiling for about 15 minutes. This gives a more homogenous mix of honey and water. And if you add fruit to your mead it will more readily absorb the fruit flavors. This heating also allows you to skim off any impurities in the honey. The one exception to this rule is if you get honey directly from a hive and it contains contaminations, wax, bee parts etc. it would be good to boil the must or the honey and skim off all the impurities.

Patience

We live in a fast paced world that is based on instant gratification. But mead making goes very much counter to this. The yeast simply needs time to transform your water and honey into wine. And as you are watching your mead do pretty much nothing you may run questions through your mind and you may doubt yourself. That is ok. But what you should do when you have questions like this is take a break, do some research, and track down some experts to help you understand before you actually do anything. The mead will be fine and it will wait for you. Don't rush to try something. There is no need for it. It is almost always better to take your time so you can make good decisions rather than act fast and make things worse.

Note Taking

If you start your batch of mead today you will not be drinking it for at least nine months to a year from now and in that time you may forget how you made the mead or what you put in it! So, what happens if it turns out great and you want to make another batch? You might not remember how you did it! Or worse, what happens if something went wrong? You might not be able to figure out what you did wrong.

So from the day you start your batch you should take notes about everything including type of water, type of honey, type of yeast, type and amount of fruit and just about everything including the average ambient temperature where you are keeping the batch.

This will help you to improve your mead making in the future. This note taking includes all the dates when you did something. Several months from now you might be wondering when you made the batch and whether or not you should bottle it. I always apply a label to the jug so the notes stay with it through the months.

Continued Learning

Mead making is a hobby, a profession, an art, and a science and this means there can be a lot to it. I recommend you continue your learning by surfing forums, checking websites, getting books, and talking to people who make mead. Your skill as a mead maker will continue to grow. I have lots of videos, tutorials, recipes, and information on my website here: www.stormthecastle.com/mead/index.htm

2 THE PROCESS, MATERIALS, AND EQUIPMENT

The whole process of mead making is pretty simple. What you are doing is adding yeast to a sugar rich environment (honey and water). The yeast loves this and grows very quickly in the mixture. As a by-product of the yeast growth carbon dioxide and alcohol are formed. You allow the carbon dioxide to escape through an airlock and voila! You have mead. Add some flavoring and you have a wide variety of meads you can make.

So, it is all about the yeast and how you care for it. And there are some rules that you have to be aware of. The yeast has a few sensitivities that you have to take care of. In this book I will guide you easily through all of these sensitivities and needs of yeast.
You will set up, make and care for your mead in ways so that none of this should be a concern. The process cares for all these different needs of the yeast. But it would be good for you to be aware of them.

The Yeast

When growing yeast and making mead there are six things to think about:

Light – yeast is sensitive to light and strong light can stop or impede a healthy growth of yeast in your mead. You avoid this by using a plastic fermentation pail, by covering your jugs and carboys with some kind of a cover, or by keeping the fermenting jugs in a dark place.

Temperature – When we think of wine we think of a cool wine cellar and this is ok after mead has been bottled and is aging for the long term but this is not a good idea for mead while it is being fermented. During the primary and secondary ferments you should keep your batch in a place where the ambient room temperature is between 65 and 75 degrees Fahrenheit (18 – 24 Celsius). If the temperature gets out of this range it can either stop or inhibit yeast growth.

Different yeasts do have differing tolerances to temperature though and if you have a question about this you should research the tolerance of the particular yeast you use; which should be as easy as looking on the package or visiting the company website.

Competition – When you create a batch of honey and water (We call this mixture "Must") you are creating an environment rich in nutrients that lots of bacteria and wild yeasts would love to grow in. But you only want your chosen yeast to grow so we have to prevent the growth of unwanted organisms. We do this by meticulously sanitizing everything that comes in contact with the must and the mead. And by pitching millions of yeast cells into the batch so it takes over fast.

Alcohol level – Alcohol is a by-product of the yeast growth and it may sound funny but it is also toxic to the yeast! After a certain alcohol level is achieved it will stop any further yeast from growing. This helps the batch by discouraging any unwanted organisms from growing and it finishes off your mead at a certain alcohol level. Each type of yeast will have a certain alcohol tolerance so if you want to tinker with the alcohol content you should choose the yeast accordingly along with the amount of honey or sugars in the batch.

Nutrients – Yeast needs food to grow and honey is what we use for this. But honey is a bit on the weak side when it comes to being food for yeast so it is advisable to supplement this with some kind of other nutrient. You can do this with fruit for a Melomel, or raisins and oranges, or preferably, some kind of commercially available nutrient that you add to the must. These commercially available wine nutrients are readily available and very inexpensive. Typically you add about a teaspoon per gallon of mead. They come in powdered form and are standard procedure for just about all wine and mead makers.

Acidity - This is something that can seem a little confusing to new mead makers but yeast has a very definite acid tolerance and your must and mead needs to stay within this tolerance or else the yeast will die off.
Honey tends to be low on the ph scale and this can cause a bit of a problem with your fermenting, or it can slow your ferment down quite a bit. We typically solve this by adding something called acid blend to the Must. It is also something readily available and very inexpensive.
Optimal ph levels are about 3.7 to 4.6 and you can easily test this with inexpensive ph test strips. A commercially available acid blend is the standard used by many wine makers but you can also adjust the ph of your batch by adding orange or citrus juice without much effect on the flavor.

In Summary: Six different things to worry about can seem like a lot but it really is very easy and taking care of all of these things is just part of the process that I will show you. In effect you just have to feed your yeast, keep it in the dark, at room temperature, nice and clean, and ph balanced.

Mead making equipment and chemicals

Let's take a look at the supplies used for mead making. I have broken this down into several sections including the basic supplies and chemicals you need to make mead, what you need to bottle it, and finally, I show you some of the more advanced equipment that is optional but nice to have.

The Basic Mead Making Equipment

Airlock – This is probably the most mysterious part of mead making. But an airlock is just a piece or two of plastic and all it does is allow gas to escape out of your fermenting mead while denying any outside contaminants to get inside. You fill an airlock half full of water.

Rubber Stoppers – These go on your jug. The solid one is so you can close off the jug and shake it vigorously. The one with the drilled hole in it is for the airlock. These come in various sizes and the typical size that you use for wine making or mead making is called a #6. If you are using a wine jug that you bought at the store the top of the jug is generally a little smaller than a wine makers jug. For this type of jug you should generally get a #5.5 rubber stopper.

One or five Gallon Jug – (You will need two of these or one of these and a fermentation pail). You can buy this at any brewery supply. If you try to use some other kind of jug just be sure ahead of time that the rubber stoppers fit snugly.

Fermentation Pail – This is not mandatory but it makes the mixing of the fruit real easy and it makes clean up afterwards very easy! You use this for the initial mixing and ferment and then the first racking goes from the pail to your glass jug. It has a hole and a rubber bung so you can place an airlock in it. They come in different sizes and the two gallon pail is perfect for a 1 gallon batch of fruit mead.

Common Kitchen Utensils – Some common utensils are good to have including a large pan for heating your honey and water, a large spoon for stirring, a funnel, a strainer if you make fruit mead, some measuring spoons and a small bowl for mixing your yeast.

Ingredients

Honey – This is the most important ingredient in your mead. While you can use just about any honey I recommend you get unprocessed honey. You can find it in grocery stores labeled as either "raw" or "unprocessed". And, If possible, you should get your honey directly from a beekeeper. This will make the best mead. The amount you should get will vary depending on your taste but I recommend to make a medium mead you get three pounds. This will be about one quart in volume. If you are making a plain unflavored mead I recommend you use an orange blossom honey and if you are making a fruit mead I recommend using a clover honey.

Yeast – You will need one packet of wine makers yeast to make a one gallon batch or two packets to make a five gallon batch. I recommend for making a fruit mead you use a champagne yeast. This is very easily bought at a brewer supply house or through an online shop like leeners.com or eckraus.com. I also have links on my website.

Fruit or spices – If you are making a fruit mead (Melomel) 1-3 pounds of fruit will be right and you can vary between this range depending on how much flavor you want in your mead. Typically I go with about 1 pound after the fruit has been cut, deseeded and de-pitted.

Water – This is not very critical and you can use tap water but if your tap water has high levels of minerals, chlorine, or other substances I recommend you get some pure filtered water.

You can use spring water but often spring water also has high mineral content. The best kind of water is the filtered kind. It is inexpensive and has almost nothing in it. It is just water.

If all you have is tap water but you are concerned about it you can boil it. This will make it better for mead making.

A look at the chemicals

You can make your mead without the addition of any kinds of chemicals and some people prefer to do just that. But there are some chemicals that are very advantageous to the process. And they are a tried and true part of the mead making and wine making process. Here is review of the more commonly used chemicals.

1. Campden Tablets – This is a chemical that will kill wild bacteria and wild yeast in your mead. It insures only your yeast will grow. Typically use 1 tablet per gallon. It is important to note that you do not add this to fermenting mead unless you want to stop the ferment. And if you use this when making your initial batch you wait 24 hours before you pitch the yeast. This allows time for the Campden to dissipate in strength so it won't kill the yeast you added.

2. Pectic Enzyme – This breaks down the pectin in fruit to bring out the flavors and it will make your mead much clearer. The pectin inside fruits can cause something called pectin haze. Typically use 1/10 to ½ teaspoon per pound of fruit. I highly recommend using this if you are making a fruit mead.

3. Yeast nutrient – This can be important for the growth of your mead. It will help insure a vigorous ferment. Yeast needs a lot of nitrogen to grow and honey is poor in nitrogen. Adding fruit

does help some but it is best to also add a nutrient. Typically use 1 teaspoon per gallon of mead. Wine nutrient will come with instruction on how much to use.

4. Wine tannin - This is often optional but it adds a certain amount of astringency and pucker to the wine. This is often more common in wines made without fruit. Typically you will use ¼ teaspoon per gallon.

5. Acid Blend – Yeast grows within a certain ph range and honey is close to out of this range. By adding acid blend you will create a better environment for your yeast to grow and you will make a better tasting mead. This will vary depending on taste and fruit used -as much as 1 teaspoon per gallon. Acid blend will vary by manufacturer so go by the directions that come with it.

6. Calcium Carbonate – this is the opposite of acid blend. It will adjust the ph of your mead if the ph is too low.

Bottling your Mead

This is a fun and rewarding part of the whole process of mead making. It is very satisfying to show off to other people your bottles of mead. You only need a few basic materials including 750ml wine bottles (standard wine bottles) some corks and a corker. There are a few different size corks you can use and I generally use #9 corks.

Labeling and waxing Your Bottles

You can finish off your bottles of mead by adding custom labels. They come in sheets that you place in your printer so you can print them up with any words, titles, or images you want. And they are adhesive backed so you can peel them and affix them to your bottles.

Another nice touch you can use to make your bottles look even better is by dipping the tops of the bottles in wax. You can purchase wine bottle wax and it comes in a wide variety of colors.

Extra equipment (Nice to Have but not mandatory)

Bottle and carboy brushes – Wine supply companies carry a wide variety of brushes for cleaning and washing wine bottles and carboys of every size. These are totally optional but very nice to have. They will make the job of cleaning and sanitizing your glassware much easier.

Hydrometer – This is a nice little tool to check the density of liquid. You can use this to gauge how your mead is progressing. Typically you take an initial reading when you first mix the must and as the sugars are transformed into alcohol the density of the mead will go down.

Ph strips – These are small paper strips that you dip into the must or mead to check the ph. This is often not necessary but is a great tool if you are having trouble with the fermenting of your mead. You can check the ph then add acid blend or calcium carbonate if needed.

Wine Thief – Is a small glass tool much like a pipette or eye dropper but larger. You dip it into your batch of mead to capture and remove a little bit so you can test it or taste it.

Corker – If you are bottling your mead you are going to need some way to get the cork firmly placed into the bottles. There are several different types of corkers and the best one, and one that I use is called a Portuguese double lever corker.

The Process: How you will make Mead

Earlier I explained the process of mead making from an overall understanding. In this part I will give you a more hands on explanation of what you do when you make mead.

This is an overview of a typical way to make mead. There are lots of variations you can apply when making mead but this is a good overview of how it is done.

Step 1: Gather all your materials and sanitize all your equipment.

Step 2: Heat your honey, half your water, and any fruits to 160° F (71 ° C) and skim off any impurities that form. Allow it to cool then put it in your fermentation pail or glass carboy. This is your must. Note that heating is optional and many people do not heat their must. I have had many great batches without heating. But I recommend that as a beginner you heat. It reduces risk of contamination, insures a very homogenous mixture of honey and water, and brings out any flavors you have added.

Step 3: Adding chemicals and more.

You add your nutrient and energizer to the must. This will feed the yeast and get it off to a good start.
You balance the acid by adding acid blend or one cup of orange juice.
If you are making a fruit mead you add a pectic enzyme and a single Campden tablet then set the batch aside for 24 hours to allow it to sanitize and dissipate in strength before you move on to step 4.

Note that both the pectic enzyme and the campden tablet are optional but good to use. I have made many batches successfully without these chemicals but I strongly recommend you use them if you are a beginner. It will increase the success of your mead.

Step 4: Starting the Yeast

Mix up a batch of yeast according to the instructions that come with it. This is usually adding yeast to ¼ cup of warm water and allowing it to sit for about 15 minutes. If there are no instructions with your yeast I recommend you gently stir the yeast into 1 cup of warm water and let it sit for fifteen minutes.

Step 5: Pitching the Yeast

You pitch the yeast into the must you made then gently stir or shake it. Put the stopper and airlock on it insuring the airlock is half filled with water.

You are now in the primary ferment stage. Within 24 hours the airlock will start bubbling. This means the yeast is starting to grow. This bubbling will get quite vigorous (more than 1 bubble per second) and it will last approximately two weeks. Toward the end of this time the airlock will slow down. Once the bubbling is less than 1 bubble every 30 seconds you are reading to rack into the secondary fermenter.

Step 6: First Racking 14-28 days from day one

You will see a thick layer of sediment on the bottom of the container. This is great sign that all is well with your mead. This is dead yeast as it goes through its normal life cycle. But it is also unwanted. At some point around the 14th day the fermenting mead will slow down. The airlock will bubble less. When this bubbling is less than one bubble every thirty seconds you are ready to siphon it into a new jug or carboy. This process is called "racking". And it gets your mead away from all that dead yeast.

You siphon most of the fluid out of your jug or pail into a new glass carboy that has been sanitized. Be sure to sanitize your siphon hose too. Leave all the sediment and fruit behind. You are now into the secondary ferment stage.

Note about variations in bubbling rate: *The bubbling rate may be different for your batch and it may slow down sooner or take longer than two weeks to slow down. These variations can be quite normal and ok. They are the result of different types of honey, different types of yeast and differences in recipes.*

If you have a question about the rate of bubbling and whether or not your mead is doing ok you should refer to the troubleshooting section of this book.

Step 7: (further racking) I typically rack my mead every month until it is clear and ready to bottle. This will take 3-6 months depending on the recipe used and the types of fruits or spices that have been added. You can rack it as often or seldom as you choose but the more you rack the clearer and crisper it will get. Some people do not like to rack at all to give the mead a thick and full body but I recommend at least one racking. It clears the mead and it also reduces the chance of something going wrong.

Optional step 8: (sweeting and adjusting taste)You can add honey or sugar to sweeten, and grape tannin to adjust pucker and astringency.

Step 9: (Stabilize and Bottle)

Typically once the airlock has completely stopped you wait another two weeks. Or if you are using a hydrometer you wait until the specific gravity has dropped about 0.100 from the initial specific gravity reading. Add a Campden tablet to kill any remaining ferment and stabilize the mead then you bottle. The Campden tablet at this point is optional but recommended..

Will Kalif

3 LET'S MAKE SOME MEAD STEP-BY-STEP

There are a lot of different ways to make mead and you could say that there is a different way for each mead maker. And this can get complex when you are talking about all the different spices and fruits that you can add to your mead. And the process for making it can vary quite a bit from what to add, when to add it, how often to rack it, and so on.

I have taken all the complexity out of this and given you five different ways to make mead. Now, this might sound like a bit much but it really isn't. You don't have to use all of these five methods. You can just pick the one that is right for you depending on your goals when it comes to mead making.

An Overview of the Five Methods of mead making

1. Faux Mead – This is not quite a real mead. This is for you if you have never tasted mead and can't get a bottle of it. So, what do you do? It will be close to a year before the real mead you make is ready to try! This method gives you a quick and easy way to use white wine and honey to make something that gives

you a sense of what mead actually tastes like. You may want to do this so you can decide whether or not you even like mead!

2. A Simple Plain Mead – This is your basic mead that uses only honey as its flavoring. You can still get a lot of variety out of this by changing the amount of honey. You can make a light, medium, or heavy.

3. A Fruit Mead – (Melomel) In my opinion this is where mead really shines. You can add all kinds of fruits to mead to make it something special. I show you how to do it and I give you rules of thumb so you can make your own fruit flavors.

4. A Spice Mead – (Metheglin) There are many different types of wonderful herbs and spices that you can add to mead and this is an art that has a long tradition including rumors of healing purposes.

5. A Sparkling Mead – (A champagne style) This is one of the biggest questions I get when it comes to mead making. How to make it sparkling like champagne? It's pretty easy to do and it is how you finish off a mead before bottling it. I show you this process and you can do this to just about any kind of the previous meads you have made.

1. Make a Faux Mead

Faux meads are made a few different ways. One way is to take an ordinary white wine and add honey to it then serve it. This has been done since ancient times and the ancient roman word for this is Mulsum. This alone is a nice way to get a taste of mead. But you can also go a step further to get a better sense of mead. It involves a little bit of heating on the stove and here is how to do it.

Ingredients:

1 liter bottle of cheap white wine

1/2 pound of honey

1 clove

a pinch each of cinnamon and nutmeg

Empty the wine and honey into a pot. Heat gently, stirring frequently, until a foam forms on the top. Scoop out and throw away the foam!

Once it has cooled you can drink it or bottle it and let it age for two weeks before drinking. The longer you leave this bottle the stronger the mead will get.

You can also adjust the strength and thickness of this mead by adding up to 1 pound of honey.

2. Make a Simple Plain Mead

Help deciding what size batch to make

You have the option of starting small with a one gallon batch or going big with a five gallon batch. The one gallon batch will yield four bottles of mead while the five gallon batch will yield approximately 20 bottles. The decision is yours and the cost is significantly different. But the recipe is almost the same and I will point out the different quantities of ingredients and chemicals that you will need for either size batch.

If you have never made mead before I recommend you go with the one gallon batch so you can learn as you go and keep your investment down. The honey, in particular can be very expensive for a five gallon batch.

An Overview of what you will do

1. Heat up your honey and water then let it cool

2. Put it into your fermentation pail or jug then add your yeast and chemicals.

3. Put the airlock on it and let it go through its initial ferment.

4. After one month you will rack (siphon) into a new container leaving all the sediment behind. This is the secondary ferment.

5. Once the secondary ferment is done you can bottle it (3-6 months) Note that more rackings may be needed if the mead is still cloudy or still forms a sediment. You would do these further rackings at monthly intervals.

6. After nine to twelve months total time since you started you can enjoy it.

A Note about the amount of honey to use: I recommend you make a medium mead which uses three pounds of honey. You can make a lighter mead by using 2 pounds of honey or a heavier mead by using 4 pounds.

Ingredients for 1 gallon batch:

- 3 pounds of honey (1 quart)
- 1 gallon of water (You won't use it all)
- 1 package of yeast (wine yeast or champagne yeast)
- 1 teaspoon of yeast energizer
- 1 teaspoon of yeast nutrient
- 1 teaspoon of acid blend
- Alternatively: You can use 1 cup of orange juice and 25 raisins rather than the energizer, nutrient and acid blend
- A Note about using energizer, nutrient, and acid blend: Often these chemicals will come with their own use instructions per gallon of wine. Use these instructions and discard my recommendations.

Ingredients for 5 gallon batch:

- 15 pounds of honey (5 quarts)
- 5 gallons of water
- 2 packets of yeast (wine yeast or champagne yeast)
- 5 teaspoons of yeast energizer
- 5 teaspoons of yeast nutrient
- 5 teaspoons of acid blend
- Alternatively you can use 4 cups of orange juice and 125 raisins rather than the energizer, nutrient and acid blend
- A Note about using energizer, nutrient, and acid blend: Often these chemicals will come with their own use instructions per gallon of wine. Use these instructions and discard my recommendations.

Equipment:

- Two glass jugs or one fermentation pail and one glass jug
- A Chemical Sanitizer like EasyClean
- A drilled rubber stopper and airlock

- Solid rubber stopper if you are using a jug for your primary ferment. If you are using a fermentation pail you do not need the solid stopper.
- A bowl for starting your yeast
- A large pan that will hold all the honey and half your water depending on whether you are making a 1 gallon mead or a 5 gallon mead.
- Some extra utensils like a large spoon or ladle for stirring and mixing the liquid
- Funnel (optional but nice)

Step One: Sanitize your Equipment

Once you have gathered together all your materials you should sanitize everything that will come in contact with the mead. This includes the jug or pail, spoon, funnel, siphon hose, rubber stoppers and anything else. Except for the pan you are heating the honey and water in. No need to sanitize that; heating up the honey/water will take care of that.

I generally do my sanitizing by filling the kitchen sink half full of water and adding the sanitizing agent.

Sanitizing is the process of cleaning all the equipment with some kind of chemical that will kill any bacteria or other types of living things. When you mix up honey and water you are creating a rich culture for the yeast to grow in. Other unwanted things could grow in it too! So, you sanitize everything to minimize this possibility.

Step Two: Creating the Must

Pour about half of your water into the pan then add all the honey. Heat this up to about 160 degrees Fahrenheit and then let it cool. You can optionally heat it to 140 F for twenty minutes then let it cool to room temperature.

You can submerge the pan in a sink with a few inches of cold water to speed up the cooling.

This mixture of honey and water is called "The Must".

Step Three: Starting the yeast

While the Must is cooling let's prepare our yeast. Typically you want to do something called "Starting" the yeast. This gets it warmed up and started before you add it to your must; and it gives you a much better chance at success.

Typically you start your yeast by gently stirring it into a cup of warm water. But your yeast might come with specific instructions right on the package. Follow these instructions. They will tell you what temperature to heat the water to and how long to let the yeast sit in the starter. If there are no instructions you can use room temperature water and let the yeast sit in it for about 15 minutes.

Step Four: Finishing the must

Using a funnel pour the must into your Jug or plastic fermentation pail. Add your energizer, nutrient, and acid blend or the recommended alternatives.

If you are using a hydrometer you can now take a reading. Be sure to write the reading down. You will need this in the future.

Step Five: Pitching the yeast

Pitch the yeast into the must and gently stir or shake it. Fill the airlock half full with water and put it through the drilled rubber stopper and place it firmly on your jug. You are done for now!

Keep it in a room or space where the ambient temperature is approximately between 65 and 75° F. If you are using a glass jug or carboy at this stage then you should place it in a dark location or cover the glass part with some kind of cloth – but do not block the airlock.

What should you do next?

After you have done your cleanup here are some of the steps to take and some things to watch out for.

Do This Immediately!

I recommend you put some kind of label on the jug, and on the label write down any relevant information. You absolutely should write the day you first made this batch. You also might want to note the type of yeast you used and the type of honey.

After 48 Hours

Within 48 hours the airlock should be bubbling. If it is bubbling then things are going very well for you. Often times the bubbling will start within a few hours.

If it doesn't start bubbling within 72 hours, something might be wrong and we need to do some troubleshooting.

- Have you kept it in a cool, dry, and dark place? If the temperature is too low the yeast might not ferment.
- Did you check the expiration date on the yeast?
-Check the airlock and rubber stopper to insure they are tightly bound onto the bottle. If something is loose the gas could simply be escaping rather than going through the airlock.
- Wait one more day and if there is still no sign of bubbling I recommend you add another package of yeast (about 1 teaspoon) then see if it starts to bubble within 48 hours.

What Is happening inside that jug?

Over the course of the next few weeks you will notice changes in the bubble rate. It will get stronger and stronger and the bubbles will come quicker and quicker then it will reach a peak and start to slow down again.

And you will notice sediment start to form on the bottom of the jug. This is perfectly normal. These are yeast cells dying off and falling to the bottom. This sediment will get quite thick and it can be as much as an inch. This is a good sign that everything is going well.

At 14 -30 Days (approximately) we move into the secondary ferment

At some point between 14 and 30 days the airlock bubbling rate will slow down significantly. Once this rate slows down to less than one bubble every thirty seconds it is time to rack the mead into a new jug.

Note if the bubbling slows down before 14 days then wait until at least the 14th day to rack. And if at 30 days the rate is still faster than one bubble every thirty seconds you should rack anyway.

How to Rack:

Racking is the technical name for siphoning all the liquid into a new jug.

Sanitize your new jug and your siphon hose then siphon all the liquid out of your jug and into your new jug. Leave all the sediment, in the old jug. The new jug should have just liquid. Move your rubber stopper and airlock over to your new jug, refill the airlock with water if needed and then set the new jug back into your cool, dark, and dry place.

I recommend you siphon it if possible, and be sure to sanitize your siphon hose! And don't try to get every last drop of liquid out of the old jug. It is ok to leave an inch of sediment and an inch of liquid in the old jug.

Try to avoid pouring the liquid

Pouring will add oxygen to the mead which is unwanted at this point. And pouring will also pour a lot of the sediment into the new jug which will alter the flavor and make it more difficult to clear it up later.

If at any point . . .

Remember: If at any point between two weeks and thirty days the airlock slows to less than 1 bubble every thirty seconds you can go ahead and rack it into a new jug. If it is still bubbling faster than this at the thirty day mark go ahead and rack it anyway.

Checking the Mead:

When you are doing this 30 day transfer you should give the mead a good smell. Does it smell yeasty, slightly alcohol, orange or ferment like? Then everything is ok. If something has gone wrong with the batch it will possibly smell rancid. This means an unwanted strain of yeast or bacteria managed to take hold – if this is the case then you should dispose of the batch and do not taste any. If it smells ok you can give it a small taste. Just to monitor it and get a sense for what it will eventually taste like.

When can you drink it?

After a month in the secondary ferment the airlock might not be bubbling much but the mead is still fermenting. I recommend that if you have a fair amount of sediment in the bottom of the jug that you rack it into a new jug once again to get it off all the sediment. You can smell it and give it a little taste at this point but it definitely needs more time. It should get drinkable at about six to nine months from when you first started the batch as labeled on the jug.

Thinking about bottling it?

You will get between three and four bottles from a gallon batch and you can bottle it. Generally, in order to bottle you wait until the airlock goes completely still with no sign of bubbling then you wait another two weeks and it should be ok to bottle. Then you wait your minimum 6-9 months from day one to enjoy it. Better to wait the 9 months to a year.

Checking with a hydrometer

You can also take regular hydrometer readings which will also tell you when the batch is ready to be bottled. Typically once the specific gravity has dropped by 0.10 the ferment is done and the mead can be bottled.

3. Make a Fruit Mead (Melomel)

A Fruit mead is called a "Melomel" and this is where I believe that mead really shines. The variety of flavors you can make is simply unlimited. If you have a favorite fruit you can probably make it into a Melomel.

It typically takes about one pound of fruit per gallon of mead. And you can vary this according to taste and experience. Some recipes call for as much as three pounds of fruit and if you have dug up a recipe that seems appealing I would recommend you go with the quantities recommended. Generally I start with one pound.

Some examples of fruits you can use to make a Melomel:
Pears, Peaches, cherries, black cherries, pumpkin, peaches, pomegranates, cranberries, raspberries, strawberries, blueberries, apricots, and well you get the idea!

An Overview of what you will do

When making fruit mead you definitely have to use a couple of different chemicals because of the fruit. These chemicals are Campden tablets and pectic enzyme. The Campden tablets will kill any wild yeast in the fruit and the pectic enzyme will break down the fruit, helping to release the flavor and prevent clouding of your mead.

Because of the use of the Campden tablet it is important to note that you make the batch of Must on one day and add all the ingredients and chemicals but not the yeast. You set the batch aside and wait 24 hours before adding the yeast.

If you added the yeast right away the tablet will kill it. But after 24 hours the potency of the tablet will have dissipated.

Optional Method – You also have an optional means of making the fruit mead. In this recipe I have you heat the fruit along with the honey and water and this is an efficient and easy way for a beginner to start out. But you also have the option of holding off on the fruit and adding it to the secondary ferment. Once the mead has finished its vigorous ferment you can add your fruit after racking into the second container. This is a good alternative that will also prevent the fruit from contaminating the batch because at this point there is usually an alcohol level of around 10% which will act as a preservative and discourage any wild bacteria from growing.

- Slice your fruit and remove seeds as possible
- Heat up your honey and half your water then remove from heat and add your fruit. Allow this mix to cool.
- Put it into your fermentation pail or jug then add your chemicals but not your yeast
- Put a solid stopper on it
- Set it aside for 24 hours to allow the Campden tablets to purify the fruit
- Start your yeast
- Pitch your yeast
- Put the airlock on it and let it go through its initial ferment
- Every month you will rack it (siphon) into a new jug if there is a layer of sediment in the jug. Once no new sediment forms you can stop racking.
- Once the secondary ferment is done you can bottle it (3-6 months) This will be either two weeks after the airlock has gone completely still or your hydrometer reads a drop of 0.10 from the initial reading
- After nine to twelve months total time since you started you can enjoy it
-

Ingredients for 1 gallon batch:

- 3 pounds of honey (1 quart)
- 1 pound of fruit (sliced and deseeded)
- 1 gallon of water
- 1 package of yeast (wine yeast or champagne yeast, or EC-1118)
- 1 teaspoon of yeast energizer
- 1 teaspoon of yeast nutrient
- 1 teaspoon of acid blend
- 1 campden tablet
- 1 teaspoon of pectic enzyme
- Alternatively: You can use 1 cup of orange juice and 25 raisins rather than the energizer, nutrient, and acid blend
- A Note about using energizer, nutrient, Campden tablets, pectic enzyme, and acid blend: Often these chemicals will come with their own use instructions per gallon of wine. Use these instructions and discard my recommendations.

Ingredients for 5 gallon batch:

- 15 pounds of honey (5 quarts)
- 5 pounds of fruit (sliced and deseeded)
- 5 gallons of water
- 2 packets of yeast (wine yeast or champagne yeast, or EC-1118)
- 5 teaspoons of yeast energizer
- 5 teaspoons of yeast nutrient
- 5 teaspoons of acid blend
- 5 campden tablets
- 5 teaspoons of pectic enzyme
- Alternatively you can use 4 cups of orange juice and 125 raisins rather than the energizer, nutrient, and acid blend

- A Note about using energizer, nutrient, Campden tablets, pectic enzyme, and acid blend: Often these chemicals will come with their own use instructions per gallon of wine. Use these instructions and discard my recommendations.

Equipment:

- Two glass jugs or one fermentation pail and one glass jug
- A Chemical Sanitizer like EasyClean
- A drilled rubber stopper and airlock
- Solid rubber stopper if you are using a jug for your primary ferment. If you are using a fermentation pail you do not need the solid stopper.
- A bowl for starting your yeast
- A large pan that will hold all the honey and half the water depending on whether you are making a 1 or a 5 gallon batch of mead.
- Some extra utensils like a large spoon or ladle for stirring and mixing the liquid
- Funnel (optional but nice)

Step One: Sanitize your Equipment

Once you have gathered together all your materials you should sanitize everything that will come in contact with the mead. This includes the jugs, spoon, funnel, siphon hose, rubber stoppers and anything else -except for the pan you are heating the honey and water in. No need to sanitize that; heating up the honey/water will take care of that.

Sanitizing is the process of cleaning all the equipment with some kind of chemical that will kill any bacteria or other types of living things. When you mix up honey and water you are creating a rich culture for the yeast to grow in. Other unwanted things could grow in it too! So, you sanitize everything to minimize this possibility.

The easiest way to do this is to fill your sink half with water and add the sanitizing agent to the water. Then soak all the various pieces of equipment you need sanitized.

I use a product called Easy Clean. This sanitizes and you don't have to rinse. You can use unscented bleach as your sanitizer. More about this in the FAQ section of this booklet.

Step Two: Make the Fruit Must ("Must" is what mead is called before you have added yeast)

Slice your fruit of choice into small pieces. If you are not using a fermentation pail the slices have to be small enough to fit into the mouth of the glass jug and more importantly they have to be small enough to easily come back out! Remove and discard any pits or seeds if practical.

Put half your water in a pan, add your three pounds of honey and heat it. Don't bring it to a boil; just heat it nicely for about ten to fifteen minutes. Optimal temperature for this is about 160 degrees Fahrenheit. Stir it regularly and skim off any foam that forms. Turn the heat off and add your fruit, stirring gently. Now let it cool. Stir it very well; you want the honey and water to become homogenous.

This purifies the honey and water, mixes it well, and draws out the flavor of the fruit.

Let that must mixture of honey, water, and fruit cool to room temperature and then get it all into your jug or your fermentation pail.

Top off your jug with water so the liquid is three inches from the very top.

If you are making this batch in a fermentation pail do not add any more water. It is difficult for you to know how much is right. When you transfer from the pail to your one gallon jug in a couple of weeks then you can top off with water.

If you are using a hydrometer this is a good time to take a reading. And be sure to write it down. This reading is called your initial specific gravity.

Step Three: Lets Add our chemicals

• Add ½ teaspoon per gallon of Pectic Enzyme into the jug. This will break down the fruit to release the flavor and it will prevent the fruit from making the mead cloudy. This cloudiness is called pectin haze.

• Add ½ teaspoon per gallon of acid blend. This will balance out the astringency of the mead and bring it into a better ph range for the yeast to grow. If you are making citrus based mead like orange, lemon or grapefruit do not add acid blend.

• Add 1 teaspoon per gallon of yeast nutrient this will supplement the food source for the yeast and keep it growing strongly.

• Add ½ teaspoon of wine tannin per gallon.

• Crush up 1 Campden Tablet per gallon and add it.

(Do Not Add Your Yeast)

Now put the stopper on this batch and shake it up mildly so all the chemicals are mixed well into the liquid. If you are using a fermentation pail you can go right ahead and stir it well.

(Note about the quantity of these chemicals: The ½ teaspoon is just a guideline. If the chemicals you purchased come with a recommended dosage then use that dosage.)

And Optional: These two chemicals are optional and you can make your batch without them but if you are a beginner I recommend you use them. It will insure a great batch.)

Step Four: (Important) Do not add the yeast at this time! You have added a Campden tablet to this batch and that is a chemical that will kill your yeast! What you have to do is keep the cork on the jug or put an airlock with water on the fermentation pail and set it aside for 24 hours. Allow the Campden tablet to do its work.

Step Five: (the following day – at least 24 hours later) Starting then Pitching the Yeast

Stir up or shake up your batch of Fruit must before pitching the yeast.

Starting is the process of warming up the yeast in an easy way so it isn't shocked when added to your must. This is rehydration of the yeast. Your yeast should come with directions on how to start it but If there are no instructions then do this:

(For a one gallon batch you will use 1 packet of yeast and for a 5 gallon batch you will use two packets of yeast.)

Stir the packet(s) of yeast into ½ cup of warm water per packet. Temperature should be around body temp. Let it sit for at least 15 minutes. It will start to become active and bubble a little bit with some froth.

Pitch the Yeast: After the minimum 15 minutes stir it then pour the whole batch into your jug or pail of Must and gently stir or shake.

Now, insert your airlock into your drilled rubber stopper, fill the airlock about half way with water and place the airlock/stopper assembly onto your jug of mead or fermentation pail. Be sure it is securely in place so the gases have to pass through the airlock and are not able to slip around the sides.

Put this in a dark place or cover the jug with a cloth and monitor it for the next couple of weeks.

What Happens Next:

Within 24 hours (often within a few hours) the airlock will start bubbling and in a couple of days it will bubble vigorously (more than 1 bubble a second). This will continue for approximately 2 weeks.

At around the two week period the airlock will have slowed down to less than 1 bubble every thirty seconds. When this occurs it will be time to rack it into a new container.

Don't forget to do this:

I recommend you put some kind of label on the jug, and on the label write down any relevant information. You absolutely should write the day you first made this batch. You also might want to note the type of yeast you used and the type of honey. And note what kind of fruit you added.

Step Six: First Racking

When the airlock slows down to less than 1 bubble every thirty seconds the primary ferment is done and it is time to rack it (siphon it) into a new container.

NOTE: If it slowed down in less than the two week period you should wait the full two weeks. If it takes longer to slow down it is quite ok; wait until it slows to less than 1 bubble every thirty seconds before you rack it.

What to do: Sanitize your new glass jug and your siphon hose and then gently siphon all the liquid out of the old container and into your new jug. Leave all the fruit and the sediment behind. Try to get as much liquid as you can but avoid the sediment!

Step Seven: More racking and finishing up several months later

You can be flexible with these guidelines but I recommend every month you rack again into a new jug, leaving all the sediment behind. If you rack every month like this it will clear up very nicely. You can stop the racking when no noticeable sediment occurs.

Bottling: As a minimum you should wait three months before bottling. A one gallon batch will yield between three and four typical wine bottles worth. A good rule of thumb for bottling is to wait until the airlock goes completely still then wait another two weeks.

Drinking: It will be a minimum of nine months since you mixed the mead until it is nice for drinking. Ideally you should wait a year. The longer you wait the better but typically it will peak somewhere between a year and two years. After that it may decline in taste –particularly if you haven't used any chemicals in the process.

Checking the Mead:

Each time you transfer the mead into a new jug by racking you should give it a good smell. Does it smell yeasty, slightly alcohol, fruity or ferment like? Then everything is probably ok. If something has gone wrong with the batch it may smell rancid. This means an unwanted strain of yeast or bacteria managed to take hold – if this is the case then you should dispose of the batch and do not taste any. If it smells ok you can give it a small taste. Just to monitor it and get a sense for what it will eventually taste like.

Using your hydrometer

If you are using a hydrometer you should be taking weekly or monthly readings. Once the specific gravity has dropped 0.10 from the initial reading the batch is ready to be bottled.

Some Final thoughts about the whole process of mead making

The yeast pretty much does all the work for you but there are two big rules when it comes to mead making. The first rule is to keep everything sanitized. Do not skip this! This is a food stuff and you will be drinking it so you don't want it to be contaminated by anything.

The second rule is not to panic! Mead needs time and it takes its time. You can also take your time. Often it is best to wait another day and monitor for a little while before taking some kind of action.

If your batch isn't bubbling in two days it will be fine to wait another day or two. And if you are anxious to drink and bottle but are not sure it will be perfectly fine to wait another week and see how it is doing; Or to wait another month before drinking it.

4. Make a Spice Mead (Metheglin)

There is a very long history to spice meads. They have been made for many centuries and they were something where the recipes were closely guarded secrets and even thought to have healing powers. Whether this is true or not is up for debate but there definitely is something to be said about Metheglins. They can be quite wonderful and they can be made using one spice or a variety of spices. This is something that you can experiment with.

Some common herbs and spices used for Metheglin making:
Cinnamon, ginger, chamomile, clover, nutmeg, parsley, rose petals, sage, spearmint, basil, tarragon, thyme, vanilla and well you get the idea!

Making the spice mix - You can add the spice directly to your batch of mead or you can brew it into a cup of herb tea. Typically you brew up one cup of hot water using the herb per gallon of mead and then pitch this into your batch of mead. There is a lot of experimentation that can be had with this and you can vary the flavor depending on taste and the strength of the herb. You can also taste the mead as it ferments and add more of your herb tea to suit your taste.

A recommended recipe:
If you are not sure what kind of spice mead to make I do have a great recipe. Per gallon of mead you use 1 cinnamon stick, 1 pinch of nutmeg, 1 whole clove, and 1 pinch of allspice. This is particularly nice holiday style mead and is great for heating up and drinking warm like toddy.

Ingredients for 1 gallon batch:
• 3 pounds of honey (1 quart)
• 1 strong brewed cup of tea made from your herb of choice (Don't use any tea leaves, just make the tea from your herb)

- 1 gallon of water
- 1 package of yeast (wine yeast or champagne yeast, or EC-1118)
- 1 teaspoon of yeast energizer
- 1 teaspoon of yeast nutrient
- 1 teaspoon of acid blend
- 1 campden tablet
- Alternatively: You can use 1 cup of orange juice and 25 raisins rather than the energizer, nutrient, and acid blend
- A Note about using energizer, nutrient, and acid blend: Often these chemicals will come with their own use instructions per gallon of wine. Use these instructions and discard my recommendations.

Ingredients for 5 gallon batch:
- 15 pounds of honey (5 quarts)
- 5 strong brewed cups of tea made from your herb of choice (Don't use tea leaves, just make the tea from your herb)
- 5 gallons of water
- 2 packets of yeast (wine yeast or champagne yeast, EC-1118)
- 5 teaspoons of yeast energizer
- 5 teaspoons of yeast nutrient
- 5 teaspoons of acid blend
- Alternatively you can use 4 cups of orange juice and 125 raisins rather than the energizer, nutrient, and acid blend
- A Note about using energizer, nutrient, and acid blend: Often these chemicals will come with their own use instructions per gallon of wine. Use these instructions and discard my recommendations.

Equipment:

- Two glass jugs or one fermentation pail and one glass jug
- A Chemical Sanitizer like EasyClean

- A drilled rubber stopper and airlock
- Solid rubber stopper if you are using a jug for your primary ferment. If you are using a fermentation pail you do not need the solid stopper.
- A bowl for starting your yeast
- A large pan that will hold all the honey and half the water depending on whether you are making a 1 or a 5 gallon batch of mead.
- Some extra utensils like a large spoon or ladle for stirring and mixing the liquid

Funnel (optional but nice)

Let's Make the Metheglin

Step One: Sanitize your Equipment

Once you have gathered together all your materials you should sanitize everything that will come in contact with the mead including the jugs, spoon, funnel, siphon hose, rubber stoppers and anything else. Except for the pan you are heating the honey and water in. There is no need to sanitize that; heating up the honey/water will take care of that. I generally do the sanitizing by filling my kitchen sink half full of water and adding the sanitizing agent.

Sanitizing is the process of cleaning all the equipment with some kind of chemical that will kill any bacteria or other types of living things. When you mix up honey and water you are creating a rich culture for the yeast to grow in. Other unwanted things could grow in it too! So, you sanitize everything to minimize this possibility.

Step Two: Creating the Must

Pour about a half-gallon of your water into the pan then add all the honey. Heat this up to about 140 degrees Fahrenheit and let it stay around that temperature for twenty minutes.

Then let it cool to room temperature. You can submerge the pan in a sink with a few inches of cold water to speed up the cooling.

This mixture of honey and water is called "The Must".

Step Three: Starting the Yeast

While the Must is cooling let's prepare our yeast. You want to do something called "starting" the yeast. This gets it warmed up and started before you add it to your must and it gives you a much better chance at success.

Typically you start your yeast by gently stirring it into a half cup of warm water. But your yeast might come with specific instructions right on the package. If this is the case then follow those instructions. They will tell you what temperature to heat the water to and how long to let the yeast sit in the starter. If there are no instructions you can use warm water and let the yeast sit in it for about 15 minutes.

Step Four: Adding the ingredients

Once the must has cooled to room temperature pour it into your jug or fermentation pail. Add your cup of homemade spice tea, your nutrient, energizer and acid blend. Or you can add your alternatives.

If you are using a Hydrometer this is a good time to take your initial reading. And be sure to write it down.

Step Five: Pitch the Yeast

It has been about fifteen minutes now so give your yeast starter a gentle stir then pour it right into the jug and either stir it gently or shake it gently. This process is called "Pitching" the yeast. You don't have to get every drop, just get most of it in there.

Step Six: Finishing

Fill your airlock half full of water, push it through your drilled stopper then put the assembly firmly onto the jug.

What should you do next?

After you have done your cleanup here are some of the steps to take and some things to watch out for.

Do This Immediately:

I recommend you put some kind of label on the jug, and on the label write down any relevant information. You absolutely should write the day you first made this batch. You also might want to note the type of yeast you used and the type of honey. And note what spices (and how much) you have added.

After 48 Hours

Within 48 hours the airlock should be bubbling briskly. If it is bubbling then things are going very well for you. Often times this bubbling will start within a few hours.

If it doesn't start bubbling within 72 hours, something might be wrong and we need to do some troubleshooting.

- Have you kept it in a cool, dry, and dark place? If the temperature is too low the yeast might not ferment.

- Did you check the expiration date on the yeast?

- Wait one more day and if still there is no sign of bubbling I recommend you add another package of yeast (about 1 teaspoon) then see if it starts to bubble within 48 hours.

There is a troubleshooting section at the end of this book if you experience problems with your ferment.

What Is happening inside that jug?

Over the course of the next few weeks you will notice changes in the bubble rate. It will get stronger and stronger and the bubbles will come quicker and quicker then it will reach a peak and start to slow down again.

And you will notice sediment start to form on the bottom of the jug. This is perfectly normal. These are yeast cells dying off and falling to the bottom. This sediment will get quite thick and it can be as much as an inch. This is a good sign that everything is going well.

Moving into the secondary ferment

At some point between 14 and 30 days the airlock bubbling rate will slow down significantly. Once this rate slows down to less than one bubble every thirty seconds it is time to rack the mead into a new jug. This moves the mead from the vigorous primary ferment into the less vigorous and much slower secondary ferment.

Note: If the bubbling slows down before 14 days then wait until at least the 14th day to rack. And if at 30 days the rate is still faster than one bubble every thirty seconds you should rack anyway.

How to Rack:

Racking is the technical name for siphoning all the liquid into a new jug.

Sanitize your new jug and your siphon hose then siphon all the liquid out of the old jug or pail and into your new jug. Leave all the sediment, the spices, the orange, the raisins, or anything else in the old jug. The new jug should have just liquid. Move your rubber stopper and airlock over to your new jug, refill the airlock with water if needed and then set the new jug back into your cool dry place.

I recommend you siphon it if possible, and be sure to sanitize your siphon hose! Don't try to get all the liquid out of the old jug. It is ok to leave an inch of sediment and an inch of liquid in the old jug. That liquid mead down at the bottom is very heavy with dead yeast so leaving some of it behind will help clear up your mead faster.

Try to avoid pouring the liquid. Pouring will add oxygen to the mead which is unwanted at this point. And pouring will also pour a lot of the sediment into the new jug which will alter the flavor and make it more difficult to clear it up later.

Remember: If at any point between two weeks and thirty days the airlock slows to less than 1 bubble every thirty seconds you can go ahead and rack it into a new jug. If it is still bubbling faster than this at the thirty day mark go ahead and rack it anyway.

Checking the Mead

When you are doing this 30 day transfer you should give the mead a good smell. Does it smell yeasty, slightly alcohol, orange or ferment like? Then everything is ok. If the batch smell rancid or putrid then it means an unwanted strain of yeast or bacteria managed to take hold – if this is the case then you should dispose of the batch and do not taste any. If it smells ok you can give it a small taste. Just to monitor it and get a sense for what it will eventually taste like.

Further Rackings

Racking is optional and some mead is made with no racking whatsoever. But I recommend you do at least one racking and the best thing you can do is rack to the needs of the mead. If at the end of any 30 day period there is a thick sediment formed I recommend you rack it. Typically two or three rackings is more than enough to clear up the mead.

When can you drink it?

. It should get drinkable at about six to nine months from when you first started the batch as labeled on the jug.

Using your hydrometer

If you are using a hydrometer you should be taking weekly or monthly readings. Once the specific gravity has dropped 0.10 from the initial reading the batch is ready to be bottled.

Thinking about bottling it?

You will get between three and four bottles from a gallon batch and you can bottle it. Generally, in order to bottle you wait until the airlock goes completely still with no sign of bubbling then you wait another two weeks and it should be ok to bottle. Then you wait your minimum 9 months from day one to enjoy it.

Some Final thoughts about the whole process of mead making

The yeast pretty much does all the work for you but there are two big rules when it comes to mead making. The first rule is to keep everything sanitized. Do not skip this! This is a food stuff and you will be drinking it so you don't want it to be contaminated by anything. The second rule is not to panic! Mead needs time and it takes its time. You can also take your time. Often it is best to wait another day and monitor for a little while before taking some kind of action. If your batch isn't bubbling in two days it will be fine to wait another day or two. And if you are anxious to drink and bottle but are not sure it will be perfectly fine to wait another week and see how it is doing; Or to wait another month before drinking it.

5. Make a Sparkling Mead

Sparkling mead is something really special. It has a bubbly and carbonated taste, feel, and look to it and it is one of my preferred methods of creating mead. It is a big hit with beginners to drinking mead much like champagne is popular to novices of wine.

Sparkling Mead - or champagne mead is just what you think it is. It is a Mead honey wine that has the same wonderful carbonated taste and consistency of a regular champagne. The process for making real easy sparkling mead is almost identical to the normal process for making mead except before you bottle your mead you stir two-thirds of a cup of honey into the batch then bottle it. (this 2/3rds cup is for a typical 5 gallon batch). Or 1/5 of a cup for a single gallon batch.

This extra honey added just before bottling will cause a small amount of further fermentation in the bottles.

But there are some cautions you should be aware of before you do this. This extra fermentation will cause quite a bit of pressure to build up in the bottles so you really need to bottle into champagne bottles because they are significantly stronger and you need to cork with champagne corks and wire caps. This is to hold the additional pressure.

Not using champagne bottles and corks can cause an explosion of the bottles because of the significant extra pressure so you really should do this to avoid injury or damage to the immediate area around where you store the bottles.

4 ADVANCED TOPICS

Bottling Your Mead

Bottling is one of the most satisfying aspects of the whole home brewing hobby. I really look forward to this part of it because it is very satisfying to see all your work, and patience, pay off in real bottles of wine or mead. It does take some equipment and some time to do so you have to slot out roughly two hours of your time to do a full five gallon carboy. Of course you will get much better at it and can bring this time down significantly with practice.

What do you need to bottle your mead?

Equipment:
• Empty Bottles (of course) clean and sanitized
• Corks - I use chamfered #9 corks
• Corking machine - I use a manual machine called a Portuguese double lever corker
• Racking cane and hose
The big issue to think about is how to get your mead from the carboy into the bottles without making a mess or spilling it. And

you don't want to handle the mead too much or slosh it around because you don't want to oxidize it. So handle it gently and easily.

You can simply use a sanitized siphon hose to get the mead into the bottles or you can use something called an auto siphon. This has a small pump on it that avoids you having to suck on the siphon which can be unsanitary.

If you are bottling a five gallon batch you may want to get something called a racking cane. This is a long solid and clear plastic tube that has a hole on the bottom. This allows you to sit the cane into the carboy and add a siphon hose. Racking canes often come in a kit along with an auto siphon. The Racking cane has a small black buffer on the bottom of it that will keep unwanted materials from the bottom of the carboy out of the siphon.

Corking the Bottles

I use a manual corker and it works just fine for me. There are more expensive corkers that will make this job much easier but I have no problem with this process. You can practice a few times on an empty bottle to get a feel for it. It really isn't that hard as long as you have the proper corks. It goes real easy if you brace the bottle between your knees or feet when applying the pressure to the handles of the corker.

I find that once the handles of the corker are fully depressed down the cork still sticks out of the bottle a small bit and you can push down on the whole corker to get the cork even further into the bottle. this is just a matter of taste and how you like your corked bottles to look.

Useful Tip: It really makes a difference if you apply pressure to the cork slowly and evenly. It will go further into the bottle.

And corks are often best if they are first steamed in boiling water to soften them up. This recommended process usually comes with the package of corks you buy.

What type of bottle should you use?

This doesn't really matter if you are making mead that is not sparkling. Just about any type of standard wine bottle will be nice. It is just a matter of aesthetics. My preference is clear Bordeaux bottles. They look good and the clear glass really shows off the beautiful color of the mead.

Alcohol content

Some guidelines and rules of thumb when it comes to percentage of alcohol in mead making

There are a couple of things that affect the end alcohol content of your mead. These are the amount of sugar content in the must (honey) and the type of yeast used.

The amount of honey you use to make your mead will have a small effect on the alcohol level. The more honey the higher the alcohol. So, dry meads will have a bit less alcohol and sweet mead a bit more.

You can always add more honey to your batch of fermenting mead after the initial ferment has finished. This will make the mead sweeter and boost up the alcohol level.

The most important factor when it comes to alcohol content in mead.

The yeast you use is the single most important factor when it comes to alcohol content. Every strain of yeast has a specific tolerance for alcohol. Once this tolerance is reached the yeast will die and the ferment will end. These tolerances are well documented and here are the figures for some of the more popular yeasts that are used in mead and wine making:

Lalvin D47   14-16%
Red Star Wyeast 3267   12-15%
Lalvin DV10   16-18%
Lalvin K1V-1116   16-18%
Wyeast 3783   11-14%
Lalvin 71B-1122   14%

If you are a beginner to mead making and you simply choose your yeast and follow standard formulas for making mead without adding extra honey you will get a pretty accurate indication of alcohol content. With adjustments for amount of honey it can vary by one or two percent either way.

With a dry mead that is light on honey the percentage would come down and with a sweet mead the percentage would go up.

One important thought about Alcohol content

If you are trying to make a dry mead with a very low alcohol content - say below 10 or 11% It will be very susceptible to going bad. Alcohol acts as a preservative and a low alcohol content makes it susceptible to contamination. You may end up with a vinegar mead!

Calculating Alcohol Content with a Hydrometer

You can get a fairly accurate calculation of the alcohol content in your mead if you take two hydrometer readings of it. The first reading should be taken when the initial must is mixed (including any fruit or spices). Take the reading before you pitch any nutrients or yeast.

And when the mead is completed and ready to drink you take a second hydrometer reading. The difference between the two measurements will give you a good indicator of how much alcohol is in it. This difference is a drop from the first reading to the second.

Here is the formula for calculating the alcohol level:

Take your final hydrometer reading and subtract it from the original reading. Then divide this by .00736. The answer is your alcohol content in percent.

Sample:

Let's say your original reading was 1.08 and your final reading is 1.01

Your subtraction gives .07

Divide this by .00736 and the alcohol content is: 9.51%

Boosting Alcohol content by freezing your mead

An artificial way to boost the alcohol content is to put the mead in a freezer safe container and freeze it. You can then remove any ice that forms. This is water content. By removing this you reduce the amount of liquid in the container but don't reduce the volume of alcohol. The result is a higher alcohol percentage.

5 RULES OF THUMB

Amount of Honey to use:
- Light Mead: 2 – 2.5 pounds of honey per gallon
- Medium Mead: 3 pounds of honey per gallon
- Heavy or Sack Mead: 4 pounds of honey per gallon

Type of Honey to use:
- Orange Blossom honey is best for a plain mead
- Clover honey is best for a fruit mead (Melomel)
- The best honey comes straight from a beekeeper

Boiling and Heating
You can make mead by boiling/heating the water and honey. Either way works well. But heating to just under boiling your water and honey mixture is optimal. It makes it more homogenous and removes impurities. Additionally, boiling the honey and water will coagulate the wax and proteins in the honey resulting in a clearer mead.

Water
The best water to use is filtered water with absolutely nothing in it. Tap and bottled water can contain high amounts of calcium, minerals or chlorine which can have an effect on the mead. And if exceedingly high they can deter yeast growth. Boil your water or let it sit for 24 hours before using if you have any question about it.

When using herbs or spices
- Generally you can brew a strong cup of tea with the herb and add that to the mead.
- Dried herbs are stronger than fresh herbs – about 2 ounces per gallon of mead is a good rule of thumb but will vary depending on taste and the strength of the herb.
- Fresh herbs are not as strong as dried herbs so you use about 2 cups of herb per gallon of mead

Will Kalif

6 FREQUENTLY ASKED QUESTIONS

How long should you keep the fruit in the jug?

This answer varies and the longer it stays in the jug the stronger the effect on the mead but. long periods of time in the jug can cause the fruit to decompose and have a negative effect on the mead. Typically two to four weeks is good for a beginner. And this will typically give just a mild flavor. You can experiment with this and leave the fruit in longer as your mead making advances.

If you are going to keep fruit in the jug for longer periods of time I recommend you treat with campden tablets and pectic enzyme.

My mead is cloudy. Is that Ok? And how do I clear it up?

Cloudy mead is normal during the fermentation cycle. But as the mead ages it should get crystal clear. If you regularly disturb the jug it will cause undue cloudiness. The best thing to do is give it time and rack it every 30 days. It will clear up as things settle to the bottom.

If after a minimum of 3 months you still want to clear your mead up some more you can use a chemical product called Bentonite. This will clear it up dramatically. Be sure to use bentonite for wine making and follow the directions. There are other types of bentonite that are not suitable for wine making.

What is racking?

This is just the technical name for siphoning the liquid (mead or must) into a new jug. It is important that you siphon and not pour so you minimize the exposure of the mead to oxygen.

What is a carboy?

This is the technical name for the glass jug that you ferment your mead in. They come in a variety of sizes including 1, 3, 5, and 6.5 gallons.

Why Do I have to use an airlock?

This is very important because while the yeast is fermenting it gives off a lot of gas and this gas will build up a tremendous amount of pressure. This pressure would pop the cork right off your jug, or worse it could literally explode the bottle or jug.

Can I do something to help protect the fruit in the jug?

Yes, you can pre-treat the fruit with a chemical called "pectic enzyme". This breaks down the fruit so it will add more flavor and it helps prevent decomposition. It will also help to avoid cloudiness in your mead. This cloudiness from fruit is called "Pectin haze".

What types of fruit can I use?

Well, you can use just about any spice or fruit you can think of. Each one is different in how it interacts with the mead so I recommend that if you have a specific fruit you want to use you peruse the internet for recipes that are tried and true. If you are experimenting with fruit I recommend you use about a cup of fruit per gallon just to get you started in your first batch or two.

How can I adjust the alcohol content?

This is definitely not something for beginners. Typically the yeast is what predominantly affects the alcohol level of the final mead. Each type of yeast will have a specific alcohol tolerance when that alcohol level is reached the yeast dies off and the batch stabilizes.

There is a thick layer of junk forming on the bottom of the jug. Is this ok?

Yes and no. It is perfectly ok that it happened- and it should happen. This layer of sediment is caused by the natural life cycle of the yeast. As it dies off new yeast grow and the dead husks accumulate on the bottom. So it is a great sign that your yeast is working correctly. But, you don't want to leave it in there throughout the whole cycle of the mead. It can cause off flavors. That is why we siphon off the liquid into a new jug and throw away the sediment.

This sediment does also have the potential of causing something called autolysis where the live yeast run out of the normal food and start feeding on the dead yeast which will cause off flavors.

How do I stop the ferment?

Well, if you want to stop the ferment so you can drink it faster I don't really recommend that. You should let the mead run its natural course. This will give you the best tasting mead. But if you really want to stop the ferment it is difficult to do. But you can come close to achieving this by adding two chemicals to the mead: potassium sorbate and potassium metabisulfite. These are inexpensive wine making chemicals that are used all the time by wineries. The combination stuns the yeast and prevents any further reproduction. So while technically it doesn't halt the ferment it does come close enough so the ferment is considered halted. Often times this is done just before bottling to insure the mead is stable before being locked into the bottle.

How do I sweeten my mead?

This is a bit of a tricky question and not necessarily for beginners but usually the mead is halted with the potassium sorbate and potassium metabisulfite combination then left to sit for two days to insure the ferment is halted. Then you add honey or sugar to it. How sweet you make it is a matter of taste but for a one gallon batch about 1/5 cup of honey should be about right. Because you have halted the ferment this process is not how you make a sparkling mead. It is just how you sweeten it.

My airlock is getting clogged with junk. Is this ok?

No, you should allow the airlock to easily breathe. Remove the airlock and stopper and siphon out an inch or two of the liquid from your carboy to give it room for bubbling. Clean and refill the airlock if needed and replace it back on the jug.

How do I know my mead is done?

Let me cover a few different parts of this. The first part is actually how do I know when my mead is ready to come out of the jug and be bottled?

There are a couple of different ways to determine this. First and best is to use a hydrometer. You take a specific gravity reading when you first mix the batch of mead. And when the specific gravity has dropped 0.1 and the airlock has stopped bubbling the batch is ready to be bottled.

If you don't have a hydrometer

You can still get a good estimation on when the mead is ready to be bottled by watching the airlock and being patient. Once the airlock has gone completely still you wait another two weeks then it should be ready to be bottled. I generally like to wait a minimum of three months.

When is the mead really done and ready to be enjoyed?

This can be a bit tricky to determine and the same goes for regular grape wines. Time is the important thing. Typically you should wait a minimum of nine months before drinking. The only sure way to know is to give it a try. And mead will often peak and go into a slow decline. It's been my experience that with most beginner meads this peak is at around the two year mark.

How much is three pounds of honey actually?

Honey varies from type to type and even from hive to hive but three pounds of honey will be about one liquid quart.

How do I use a hydrometer?

A hydrometer is simply a bobbing tool with lines on it. It will come with instructions on how to use it. You take a sample of your mead and put it in a container (it comes with the hydrometer) and just drop the hydrometer right into the container and read the number at the top of the mead line. Simple as that. The hydrometer just reads the density of the liquid. The denser the liquid the higher the hydrometer will float.

7 TROUBLESHOOTING YOUR MEAD

Your Batch of mead doesn't appear to be fermenting or the airlock is bubbling very slowly.

If this is your first batch of mead you might be wondering about the airlock and how much it should bubble.

Normal bubbling

Within the first 24-48 hours after you added the yeast the airlock should start a slow bubbling – maybe 1 bubble every 30-60 seconds. Then over the course of the next 2-3 weeks the bubbling will get vigorous (more than 1 bubble a second). If these things don't happen you will need to troubleshoot your mead.

Here are some guidelines for troubleshooting.

1. Did you add Campden Tablets to your mead? If so, did you wait at least 24 hours before adding the yeast? If you did not then you should add more yeast to the batch. The Campden Tablets probably killed your yeast. Add the same type of yeast and same quantity as you did when first making the batch.

2. Did you check the expiration date on your yeast? Yeast can last a long time but it does expire. If the yeast has expired then add more yeast in the same type and quantity you originally used.

3. What is the temperature of the room that you are storing the mead? If it is below 65 F (18 C) then it might be too cold and your ferment has stalled. Move the mead into a warmer location and it may start up. If it doesn't start up you should follow other guidelines for troubleshooting.

4. Check the PH of your mead. Honey is low in ph and the Must may be out of the growing range for your yeast. Use small

paper ph strips to check the acidity. If it is below 3.7 then add calcium carbonate blend to the must and then see if it starts up within 24 hours. If the ph is over 4.6 then add acid blend and see if it starts up within 24 hours. If not then pitch a new batch of yeast. Alternately you can add a half cup of orange juice per gallon and re-check the ph.

5. Is your must being kept in a dark place or has it been covered? Light, and particularly sunlight, can prohibit the yeast from growing. Put a cover on your jug being careful not to block the airlock, and see if the ferment starts bubbling within 24 hours. If it doesn't start up then refer to the other troubleshooting steps.

6. Food for the yeast – Did you make a recipe that doesn't use some type of supplemental food for the yeast? I mean is there no fruit, energizer, nutrient, raisins, tea leaves or anything else? Is it just honey, water and yeast? Honey is a borderline poor food for yeast and you might want to just add a handful of raisins (25 per gallon of mead) or some wine maker's nutrient (it comes with quantity recommendations). Wait 24 hours to see if the ferment starts up and if it doesn't then you can pitch more yeast.

If your mead just won't clear up

If you are having trouble getting your mead to clear up you can use a product called bentonite which will clear it right up. It is an inexpensive clay product and it comes with instructions for use.

8 DEFINITIONS AND MEAD MAKING TERMINOLOGY

Racking – The process of moving the liquid in a container of mead into a new container. Typically this is done by siphoning.

Carboy – A glass container for fermenting. They come in a wide variety of sizes ranging from 1 gallon to 6. 5 gallon.

Primary ferment – This is the first period of mead ferment just after the yeast has been added. This ferment is typically very vigorous and lasts 2 – 4 weeks.

Secondary ferment - This is a longer and slower ferment period. The yeast is still growing but at a slower rate. This period can last several months.

Pitching the Yeast – The technical term for adding your yeast to the must.

Headspace – This is the amount of air at the top of a container or carboy above the mead. It is generally advisable to keep this space to a minimum because of the risk of oxidizing the mead. You can add distilled water at any point to minimize this space.

Lees – The dead yeast that accumulates at the bottom of a fermenting batch of mead (sediment).

Specific Gravity - This is a reading of the density of a liquid. Water has a specific gravity of 1.000 and it is a reference point for other liquids. As you add fruits, honey and other things to your mead the liquid gets denser and the specific gravity goes up. As the yeast metabolizes the honey and fruits, transforming it to alcohol, the specific gravity will drop closer and closer to 1.000. This is a good way to know if your mead is fermenting and when it is done.

Must – The technical term for your batch of mead before you have pitched the yeast into it.

Pectin – a substance in fruits that is very jelly like. It can be difficult for the yeast to break down and it can cause a haze in the mead. Using pectic enzyme aids the breakdown process.

Short Mead - A general term for a fast fermenting mead that ages quickly. Typically it is achieved with an aggressive yeast and a light amount of honey. Short meads are often very ale like.

Hydrometer – This is a glass tool for measuring the specific gravity of a liquid. It is much like a fishing bob with measurements on it. You drop it in the liquid and it floats then you read the measurement by looking at the numbers on it.

9 FURTHER RESOURCES

Website: I have a tremendous amount of material on my website all about mead making; recipes, processes, articles and a lot mead making tutorials.

www.stormthecastle.com/mead/index.htm

Videos: On my youtube channel I have many video tutorials that show you how to make mead from start to finish and many other things like how to rack, how to bottle, and how to clarify your mead. From my youtube channel look for the playlist called "Mead Making". www.youtube.com/user/epicfantasy

E-books: I currently have two eBooks that give you a fast and easy process for making mead either plain or fruit. The eBooks take you through the process as I make a batch of mead and explain it all step-by-step with pictures. www.stormthecastle.com/mead/index.htm

Will Kalif

INDEX

ABOUT THE AUTHOR

Will Kalif is a writer and webmaster. He has been making mead for many years and it all started out of his simply wanting to try mead and not being able to buy any! He has made more batches than he can count and has made some terrific meads while having some enormous five gallon disasters along the way. You can visit his website at: www.stormthecastle.com

Made in the USA
Middletown, DE
03 December 2015